DOLL HOUSE MASQUERADE

poems by samuel e. cole

TRUTH SERUM PRESS

Also by Samuel E. Cole

Bereft and the Same-Sex Heart (poetry)

Bloodwork (short stories)

Siren Stitches (short stories)

TRUTH SERUM PRESS

Truth Serum Press
32 Meredith Street
Sefton Park   SA   5083
Australia

Email: truthserumpress@live.com.au
Website: http://truthserumpress.net
Truth Serum Press catalogue: http://truthserumpress.net/catalogue/

Cover design by Matt Potter
Author photograph © Jean Hoffman

ISBN: 978-1-925536-43-0
Also available as an eBook / ISBN: 978-1-925536-44-7

Truth Serum Press is a member of the
Bequem Publishing collective
http://www.bequempublishing.com/

For

My Dad & Siblings

Contents

Intelligence

Cherry Horses

Like the hunger we discovered
inside a barn with a picture window shut tight,
making love with unmasked fervor because
transparency to boys who willingly linger

in the scrub are birds riding the wind
through lime trees deep in the dunes
above the proof of existence: retracing every
regret: we've been there. But what of you, enticed,

enthralled, entranced with how a song
becomes its own myth and religion: out from the dark,
polished in the tube of a throat, so stubborn.
I know what it's like to lie sleepless in your brook,

both as the willow (and) as the gardener,
scrawled on a wall of ivy behind something
performed in the service of truth. Already beaten.
Lying naked on a bamboo mat, we felt

our hearts stop searching for instructions, day
after day, chamber by chamber, the high notes descending.
I can live in flotsam and dirt, though
I won't get far: a storm howling with

beauty is the aftermath
wrestling through the pale wings of morning
breaking into your arms. I remember
there are many kinds of hunger,

but it would make no difference. Every sequence,
in every city, all one the earth, even the
shining in the hair at the nape of your neck, the dark
back of the curve held in by itself finds us scurrying away,

removing ourselves from the bossy,
because those not found
form sounds in such a way
as all we did was wait there. Keeping vigil.

A Most Promising Boyfriend's Daughter's Perspective

He's not mother's replacement. Nor a step-father.
Nor commonplace among friends. Or family.
Society is friendlier, for sure. But still. Not
everybody approves. Or gets it. Mom

remains quiet, throwing snark-bombs in
the annual Christmas letter—the best place
for gay to come out and own its truth

among the sassy spirits of the season.
Where (and when) did Dad meet him?
They speak gym, Trivago, NFL, Herberger's.
They hold hands in the car, on the street,

at the store, during movies. If Dad held Mom's hand,
I don't remember, nor do I understand man-crush
softness—*hey there cutie-sweets*—which pains
me for Mom, who isn't dating, nor is she soft,

marinating poorly in Dad's fiery, rejection stew.
Perhaps this is why she does not hug me.
Nor my brother. Too many one-sided questions of intimacy
she cannot toss aside or hold too close. I get it.

Detach from any genetic reminder of who
he is. Or was. I do not blame her. Nor do I pry.
My dad is honest so I believe he did not trick her.
He is kind so I believe he did not mistreat her.

He is solid so I believe he did not intend to
leave her hollow, moving around the house as if
everything within it is a misplaced nickname.
My dad is happy so I believe he does not regret

taking the risk of moving on. And out. My brother
agrees, adds eye-rolls, wrist-flicks, & stereotype-slurs.
My dad is anti-typecast, quite unlike his…spouse?
Friends ask if I (she, we) feel betrayed, lied to,

bamboozled, eclipsed. I do not. And why should I?
Like Dad, and Mom, I also enjoy watching a novelty
act reach the zenith of its dwindling attractiveness.

Instinct

serious psoriasis / serious eyebrows
higher, higher, higher
I was five and secretly wondered
if my mother was a crater / if my father was a scarecrow
let off from some planet / let off from some hook
by a
vanilla queen / hairstylist king
who
rejected and cast out / plucked and shaped
scary things
it could not stand
to recast / to reshape
was father's accusation when he / was mother's accusation when she
thought my ears lay dreaming
in clean silence—in bed—
but I was awake, heartbeat adrift
among the sounds of
cosmic collision

teakettle whistling / fireplace crackling
sizzling firefly lights / barking neighbor Dalmatians
squeezing my face deep into / beating the back of my head into
the pillow
casting worries
toward
a painted fish / a hunting knife
silken scales and a clear tail / silver glint and a sharp tip
sketching a white line,
a swirl of motion
swimming away / carving away
lower, lower, lower
to another planet / to another hook
far below
the creamy luster of the moon / the scraggly aspens in the woods

Twin Hands

I am (dis)pleased with six arriving
twice a day and (mid)night

only once. It is (un)fair
when smaller things supplant

bigger things and are then
reprieved of any responsibility

of (know)able (wrong)doing.
Oh, the (in)opportunity of youth.

Epiglottis

Cloaked in a dense, sooty haze,
chimney fires blazing
skylines to earthworms,

record coldness outlasting
lower rung wood prices and
fresh food and it's a near

impossibility for death to not
wail multitude horrors
filling the dark corners

of the city's labyrinth streets,
penniless masses huddled like
a giant coat splayed without

buttons, braids, or beauty,
because faithfulness is not yet as
important as straight. Close. Coming.

Bring scissors, tape, and finer needles.
Gods like their fashion tidy. Like their followers.
Like the robes holy-smoke men swish upstairs

far from soot, earthworms, and corners;
far from wound-scabbed hushmarks
rumbling across the bridge,

looking neither at the river nor at the poverty,
too busy fraternizing with other transfusionists
cloaked in a dense, sooty haze.

Sister Interruption
via Smartphone

She cries on the phone her children are lost,
daytime and nighttime, always in season.
It's sad but sadly they've always been lost.

Her daughter keeps rounding, fifteen years lost,
can't reach the suitor, only the treason,
she cries on the phone her children are lost.

Her oldest keeps sobbing, sixteen years lost,
classmates throw insults at kinfolk gone wrong.
It's sad but sadly they've always been lost.

Her son falls behind, no paradise lost,
cheating binds breakdown to schoolyard bongs,
she cries on the phone her children are lost.

Her youngest admits to feeling so lost,
fat, cunt, and ugly, Miss Pointless Dumb-Fuck.
It's sad but sadly they've always been lost.

Her husband agrees, "I'm worried we've lost.
Where is our future and what will it cost?"
She cries on the phone her children are lost.
It's sad but sadly they've always been lost.

Fundamentality

The torment enunciating
life without you

is an ineluctably afoul
adverb redefining every

improper noun

concealed from every
helping verb we didn't link.

Mars Ambassador

He believes it: sometimes
a thing can be star-like,
a middling weight or
a great feat until, by winter,

it leafs out of season.
Ash Wednesday is calendar X,

loose leaflets of God,
(he believes) holy words are
an instrument of negotiation.
See: Jesus is a power broker.

Read (his) correspondence, yes,
how superior are the purifications
of discernment when surpassingly
reached by way of delivering

2000 years, he preaches, foot on his name,
ripped muzzle, pressed against

history fooling the goldenrod—
now even (his) eyes have
dedicated powers hooking
and trapping me like a

spider weaving a blackened web.

And when (he kneels) in phosphates
of hemlock and error,
he fills my eyes with
vast holes, OMG, I'm inside a

single molecule of abandon—
And so is the spider, & yet (his)
variations help him forget
the space between a blink,

how the infinite mixes of dyes
swirl along the way
(please don't bite or chew)

bumping me from the WORD-perch
to wash the base of this street.

The Opposite of Undone

Our partnership was
entwined in a slip

knot known more for
being jumbled than tight.

Residence Booster

If you ever came over,
which you can't, I'm sorry,
I think you'd like my new home.
I've named him Lance. Full name: *Relancement.*
A French Tudor—tres darling: tres sweetie: tres mine:
who enjoys interior design, sharing, and sustainability.
My new neighbor-friend, Ben, a rambler-jokester,
says if I'm not careful, goddamn it,
Lance and I are going to merge into
a wonderful world of wholeness.
Ben also went through a painful breakup,
which is why I think he's a jokester,
and also why he so often says *goddamn it.*
I understand goddamn it—
It's more fun to swear in pain than to seethe alone.
"I'm jealous of you and Lance," Ben says.
Ben's heart, like his house, needs TLC.
Every room is a gridlock of soot, junk, & rust.
You and Ben share a commonality:
you both collect toys, play with them for
a spell, set them aside, & forget they exist.
Ben likes to ramble on about remodeling,

but I have yet to stumble upon one tool,
one paint swatch, one décor magazine,
one family picture—something to prove
he's serious about wanting to change.
Last week, during a Sunday run
—we both want to shed a few pounds—
I tiptoed around some twiggy remnants
of an abandoned bird's nest, when Ben said,
"Imagine the fucked-up shape of its inhabitants.
I bet they're dead, and happier because of it."
I worry Ben's suicidal. I hope he finds a job soon.
Hopelessness is the most twisted branch of poverty.
Ben believes neither in self-regulation nor in
gun control. He doesn't know that a few months
ago I pressed the tip of a gun to my chest, dotted
the shape of a heart, teased the trigger, & waded in
the energy of its purposefulness. But I couldn't buy
a bullet, so I returned the gun and bought
a pair of scissors with which I cut from
red cardstock a large heart & wrote in thick black
marker inarguable cardiovascular facts, like the
circulatory system removes waste, fights
infection, & delivers nutrients to the body.
I taped the red heart to the front door. Ben
mocked the red heart, but left it alone.
"The heart beats one hundred thousand
times in one day," I told him. Over and over.
"That's one hundred thousand more

beats then I want in one day," he said. Again and again.
I know he's hurting. His eyes constantly water.
His limbs constantly twitch. His ass constantly sits.
He enters my house without invitation,
moving freely about the rooms:
manhandling doorknobs, light
switches, remote controls, window
blinds, and the pull-out sofa-bed inside the
couch on which he can, and does, sleep and
snore for days. He also likes to rearrange the
self-help hardcover books on the coffee table.
"You need to mess things up," he says.
"Perfection's an abnormality and self-help
is total bullshit. How can you buy into it?"
"Self-help means healing," I say every time.
"Self-help means zilch," he says every time,
slamming the door, rattling the red heart taped
to the front door. I hope it doesn't fall off.
But if it does, I will tape it back up.
"Ben means to kill you," Lance says. Over and over.
"I wish he'd move away, and stay away forever."
I'm perplexed. I like Ben. And we are losing weight.
And he is funny. And I do appreciate the camaraderie.
I fear if I lose him, I won't be able to help him.
Sometimes I lie down in the den and seep my
fingers deep into Lance's brown, curlicue
chest hair and rest my face against the
tight weaves. He never pushes me away

or yells get the fuck out of my hair.
Sometimes we fool around for hours.
He seems to like my touch. So far.
Lance, however, avoids the kitchen,
and he hates to cook. I thought all French
Tudors loved kitchens and cooking.
So did Ben. Neither of us can remember
a time when we didn't believe that to be true.
It's comical—human bias, I mean—how we
instinctively assume others will become
the realization of our expectation.
Last week, after Ben went home, and after
I rearranged the books on the coffee table
and pushed the sofa bed back into the couch,
I told Lance, *I don't like to cook either,*
tres darling. Eating out's way more fun.
Lance laughed for five minutes.
What's so funny? I asked.
You said eating out.
I laughed, too. For six minutes.
We couldn't stop laughing.
Then, as if reading my mind, Lance
whispered something of such resonance,
I cried for ten (or was it thirty?) minutes.
Neither of us, in this kitchen or the next, will
ever be beaten, pounded, or ground into bits.
I believe the last owner really hurt Lance.
Yes, I thought about phoning you, to tell you

about Lance, about Ben, about the Sunday runs,
about the guilt of suicide, about missing you,
and to ask if you wanted to come over,
which I can't, I'm sorry, I won't jeopardize
what Lance and I are building with what you
and I destroyed. We all deserve better.
Every night, after Lance is tucked in bed
and the sheep are grazing, I quietly
sing *This Old Man* as I trace a finger
along a red laceration line that starts above
the fireplace and dips across the
dining room and widens in the stairwell
and comes to form a triangle above
a small, square window in the attic
—the last owner was fond of knives—
where I face the moon, osmosis and wax,
and hope for Ben's rambler-jokester,
reimagine Lance's red laceration line,
confess our multitudinous mistakes,
and reach for your heart, wherever it may be.

Good Housekeeping

We pick at laundry
the way we pick at hate—

take what's ours—
fold it in half—

put it away to
wear another day—

Toyland

half the time, I tweak my chest to absorb the pressure of his
covering: thick gray hairs,
modern and magnanimous, blasting my heart with bumps
and spells—

some of the time, I beg his face to worship the cells in my
hands: thick white lines,
euphoria and ascension, caressing his cheeks with strums
and wisps—

all the time, I move a torrent of clocks to trespass and
rewind: thick black levers,
firm and exploration, linking our curious rhythms with
stains and tears—

The (UN)Musicality
of Miscellaneous Romance

consider me the online post
your vexing sleeplessness was
meant to click on, turning isolation's

unsettling jam one degree closer to
the smooth groove you keep telling
yourself you can't live without—

Not anymore.
It's time to boogie.

Now that you're hooked, relax.
Surrender to yes. Unwind.
Perhaps together we can turn

our genres into a chart-topping
love song. I compose a lush,
melodic rhythm boosted by a

surprisingly tight bridge, and if you
strum the merriment of harmony
and enjoy blending strings

to notes and margins to riffs,
let's collaborate. Why not chart the
score we've been playing by ear. So far.

Ad-libbing is for slapstick comedy.
Arrangement is serious business.

Now ask yourself whether the ring-
tone of curiosity or the reprise of
skepticism is enticing you to proceed.

There's no wrong answer. This is Craigslist
after all, the orchestra-pit of curiosity and
skepticism. If your heartbeat is rumbling
like teeming kettledrums, why not flavor the

cadence with a syncopated bass line. Jazz it up.
Lengthen the mix. Reply. Help us avoid
becoming a one hit wonder. First, strike the

porn site distracting your attention
(at least minimize it), retract the nakedness
(tight boxers will do), twist open the window

blinds (moonlight is the new popstar), and soak
up my euphonic verve wafting like a classical acoustic
guitar. What you want to avoid is settling-for.

But we can talk about that after Vivaldi. In bed.
Now it's time for resounding reconfiguration.

Has my little opus found the right
audience? Someone who gets it? Really?
Add to my tempo grin, fashion-height hair,

olive eyes, 5'10, 182.8, DDF, Keurig, jogger,
blogger, STEP-evolver, NFL, Marvel, H&M,
type-A, Sill-A, no-pets, no pigs, no cigs,

you have an underscore with ballad capabilities.
A rough draft in need of a final revision.
Matter in search of form. Modernism calling out to

Lucky Charms, French Kissing, and Fantasy Island
to come home. A whisper to the troposphere
to count, to stream, to trend, to dance, to belong.

"Amazeballs post," you'll respond. "Let's hang."
"I like amazeballs," I'll respond. "A lot. I'm in."

We schedule a meet-and-greet at Glam Doll
Donuts in Minneapolis where we'll sip coffee
and share two cake pastries—The Peek-A-Boo

and The Darling?—laughing like electric trombones
across a metal-hooved table at first-hi newness,
hot jokes, modulation, and instrument preferences,

and I'll admit to feeling like a piano, uncertain
of my grandness or if I hold any melody or if
I want another's man's fingers pressing my keys or

if I can recall any register beyond the dirge of blues.
And there will be friction in my voice and we'll linger
like intermission in the diminuendo of my tenor
as I admit to not wanting to be a piano but a
vibrato-harmonica with so many purling glory holes.
And we'll giggle and walk to ours cars after you

mention an affinity for arpeggio and for tickling
ivory and you'll ask if I too, like a good musical revival
on Broadway, feel the surge of pride that
comes with putting myself out there again.

Not entirely, I'll say.
But I do believe in practice.

Memory

The Beginning Stages
of Connecting the Dots

Your left arm scar shaped
like a Titanoboa snake slithering
down a bone-shy ravine shoulder
to elbow bit me halfway

around September Lake, jogging
shirtless in rainbow-frayed
board shorts, sweating out
last night's karaoke-picks,

ale-rounds, and midnight diners,
working hard to stitch
distance fears into boyfriend
paradise craving permanency

of excess. "What happened?"
I asked coyly, though I am not,
outsider boldness tempered
only by animalistic gravity.

"Oh that," you said, redressing
the rift. "It's nothing. Really.
Don't worry. I'm better. I'm fine."
"Does it hurt?" I asked,

looking for any reason
to touch you, to trace the cobra,
to fill the ravine, to get
close and stay closer, to become

salve-healing administered
through constant contact.
"Sarcoma at seventeen," you said,
restarting the jog, rousing silence

except for the bottom of
tennis shoes scuffing rebel dirt
specters creeping like parked
cars in a cement lot flanked by

spotless ponds and smooth trees
lined with idyllic bark and vines.

You waved goodbye with your
right arm, keeping hidden for five
thousand moons rougher, more
malignant mutilations mutating within.

Born This Way

if simplicity had birthed in me an extra
C, an extra chrome, an extra please...

if innocence had grown plus bone
a straighter me, an easier sea...

if dependence walked in shadow glands
and the only choice was to hold my hands...

if spoken tongue was slow and fair
and every path led motives bare...

if self was less and less was more
and more was less than a closing door...

if trust relied was trust applied,
I'd choose such trust with you in mind...

if I was down with pattern gene,
might I belong to you and me...

Never Gonna Give You Up, Never Gonna Let You Down

1.

Evening before the junior high Shimmy-Shake Costume
Dance, thunder cursing farmyard stink, a fake cough
hacking in the den—pure heresy—alarming neither my
spruce-tree father nor thorn-bush mother nor wild-grass
siblings who pulled at each other's roots before inserting
their New Boonies into the family van, off to see another
holy ghost tambourine show where drunk-on-Jesus
levitation altar calls and big city choir hair bringing
enchantment to kith bound tightly to whirlwind godliness. I
knew there was no song, dance, or moonlight hex to cure
the secret, closet conversations between me and my bizarro
ball-and-socket-joint machinations.
I was that kind of naivety.

2.

Hours alone were mine to mine the garb of people with
paying gigs: snatched my sister's Rick Astley t-shirt and
L'eggs sheer energy webbed stockings and lashed L'Oreal
Paris black eyeliner and swished red fingernail polish and

doused my brother's leather jacket and checkered Vans
with Paul Sebastian cologne and spray painted plum lines
on white jeans and cut and taped a sandpaper belt and
marked pink triangles on my earlobes and detailed orange
cones on my knuckles and blistered my tongue on
expletives sure to add cool points to this fantastic cavalcade:
goddamn it, if I didn't mirror my own wow.
I was that kind of reconnaissance.

3.

Every rite of passage needs embellishment bling, but
mother's Tourmaline rings choked my fingers and father's
hair gel felt as dense as a JCPenney church suit. Their
wears, like their marriage, held nothing but antiquated
uselessness. Their bathroom stunk of yellow toilet water.
Gray crust tracked the bathtub. The linoleum floor rolled in
on itself. The medicine cabinet sequestered dirty Q-tips and
hand-squeezed tubes of ointment with funky stage names:
Asper Crème; Mo-Bisyl; Poly-Myxin. I jumped on the
mattress and straightened above the headboard a large
square picture of two peony's shooting like springtime from
mother earth (or is it father time?). I outlined with a finger
a crack in the glass. I wiped an inch of dust from the top
frame. I counted ten toe prints and a bazillion fissures on
the footboard.
I was that kind of microscope.

4.

Home at midnight from Jesus Fest 7.6, father and mother
argued about which prophets best heal sicko queers and
gutted pro-lifers while my siblings played Uno, Racko, and
Twister in the backyard.
I was that kind of phantom.

5.

Night of the dance, father drove the speed limit to the
school doors where testosterone and estrogen gathered like
rambler cells emoting pretty to swells and me falling
somewhere at the end of neither. I jumped out and primped.
Father honked and made a u-turn. *Here's five dollars. See
you at ten. Don't forget son, Jesus is always watching.*
I was that kind of going rate.

6.

Patrickgregkeithpauljasonbriankarltonywaynerolandjeremi
ahlanceterryjerryindianaevenhector
emblazoned similarity black ties and Midwestern boot-cut
jeans while buzz-cut Pam-moo-lah squeezed my hand &
did the breaststroke through groupie-clan maws spewing
freak, weirdo, sissy, homo, queer: curses thrown like
spikes; labels wet with spittle; parallels chasing away
differences; normality voicing its aggravation against
abnormality. "It gets better" & YouTube had not yet been
invented. The future was now and praise-be-to-Pam-moo-

lah for being a butch-hag, a battle cry, a shield, an athletic
supporter, a checkmate, a friend.
I was that kind of player.

7.
Pam-moo-lah howled at my thigh-high stockings and I
howled at her father's camouflage underwear: textures
implanted by definition into our chromosomes. Years later,
as the dyke and the queen, we'd laugh so hard we'd cry
until the hardness cocooned around our hearts softened the
tear ducts we had no choice but to blink away.
I was that kind of confession.

8.
The gymnasium thumped and rattled to Culture Club.
Dead or Alive. Wham! Frankie Goes to Hollywood.
Queen. Madonna. Cyndi Lauper. Tears for Fears. Rick
fucking Astley. *Never gonna give you up*, we sang. *Never
gonna let you down. Never gonna run around and desert
you.*
I was that kind of dreamer.

9.
Mrs. Snorek complimented my freshness. Mr. Fink asked
about my mother. Principal Pol sighed.
Miss Camacho said, *Hola Samuel.* Pam-moo-lah and Janet
Louise Hastings clasped hands while

Leejohnivanscottthomasleifdavidjoemarkrogerdalestevekyl
ecarltonrayrobnevadaevenlejjarious
held me prisoner by their off-limits allure growing strong
like a wild animal tracking a scent that ends in a trap, so I
kicked open the third floor bathroom stall at 8:30 and
gasped—etched in knife-font scrawl on the wall was my
phone number - CALL FOR A BJ. I rearranged the letters
in my head, to make it funny, to make it not true, to make it
stop. Stop. Stop. The fake cough reappeared, worse than
ever, hoarse. I phoned home and crashed Pam-moo-lah and
Janet's make out session on second base. *You become the
absurdity their slander campaign wants if you can't learn to
let it go*, Pam-moo-lah and Janet spoke in unison. Lipstick
leeches. Father sniffled during the drive home where
mother and siblings walked circles around me.
I was that kind of livestock.

10.
I threw Rick Astley against the wall, a first headache of
many to come.
A first encounter with rage. And with Satan, God's hottest
boy-toy.
I lied in nakedness face down on the mattress and ceded to
the disease of darkness.
I was that kind of gay.

Going Gray

Grandfather's fingers
swallowed the bitter

branch of sorrow—
I am leaving—

mourning can be
such a letdown—

termites breeding
in the bathwater—

And now,
from a better place,

there's no one
left to see our hands.

Cyclical Realizations

"I'm so depressed," man one whispers. God, he hates this feeling.

"Give it some time," man two says, standing in front of him like an ill-fit garment looming in the back rack of a closet's imagination.

Man one buries his head in the center of man two's fluffy, red jacket. Like always, man two's wood-scented cologne ripples man one's skin with goose bumps. Man two kneels and cracks a knee. "Is there anything I can get you before I leave?"

They linger in silence. So many things neither get.

Man two stands and swipes a finger across man one's chin. "Maybe a drink?" He drums with light, tight fists the width of man one's shoulders. "I put the dry cleaning slip on the washing machine. They have like two bags worth of your stuff."

Man one studies his toenails, wondering if dead skin, even alive, is more dead than alive.

"Alrighty then," man two says—man one can hear him so clearly—shutting the garage door and driving away.

Man one hates silence: curses it, as if to remind the air, the ceiling, and the empty engagement frame hanging crooked on the wall that man two isn't coming back, at least not to him.

Me and Daddy, Now

—Jesus loves you, son.
—Don't forget the blood of the cross.
I played the message over and over,
his voice full of disputation:
—I felt the call of God to phone and remind.
—I need to tell you one more time.
I phoned back, screamed Jesus Schmesus!
—why can't you just say hi?
—why does everything have to include him?
He groaned.
—You've become so lost and hard-hearted.
—You're not the man redemption requires.
—Good only comes to those who love the Lord.
—Rebellion is as the sin of witchcraft.
—You are void of heaven's praise.
He paused to cough and swallow.
I hung up and didn't phone back,
didn't ask are you okay, nor when (or why) the cough.
Enjoy purgatory and wave upward, hypocrite.
And now the chance is over
to phone and whisper
—are we okay?
—I hurt.
—I care.
—I love.

Me and Daddy, Then

Legs scissoring the progression
of backyard races with sweet amusement
as summer thrills brought playoffs
before the coming crunch of fall,
more dust than yards away
I eyed the rope-swing-goal
beckoning calf muscles
to bend and stretch
my ten-year head ahead
might just be mine to win and taunt
in dance and claps
I told you so…I told you so…
but I couldn't match his faster feet
or outreach his feather arms
or tie his signature fingertips
breaking the rope-swing-goal—the victor—
I frowned, breathless, mulled, begging for a re-run, a redo.
Oh-no, he said, *I've won, you've lost, all's fair, it's done.*
And I couldn't swallow the pintsize bite of imbalance, nor
understand how
a father can caste a son a loser & berate
in subsequent years
witchcraft sin nullifying heaven's praise
with taunts & dance & claps

I'm Just Saying

A flower
offers little scent
to a predetermined
mind.

Countermeasure

Around here,
dirt stands on the porch
like yard sale scuffmarks—

old cows sucking
barn-burning jaundice
with dizzying breadth—

seeded threats
becoming someone

else's underbrush:
a sad little ribcage
carpets the halls of my body

King for a Day

another spin growing up
two words rarely spoken

at bedtime by sapped parents
with heavier goals than to raise

my yearly trance of wishing
for splendidness filled with

easy minutes eating strawberry
ice cream and gooey

chocolate cake with metal
silverware on funky dessert

plates while galaxy voices
sprayed three words

overwhelming me like a
rain shower:
we love you…

no four—no five—
sweet son

Empty Vessels

I can bring a photograph
into sunlight steam, flamboyant

colors migrating to coiling corners,
glitter plaids & SKOL caps

centering the moment of
our annual-VACA history,

a locomotion steamrolls through Dublin,
red-metal Guinness emblazoned on both sides,

the *sniffy-liffy* bears down on blueprint
tourists—follow the signs: the shadows: the scents—

& as I shake my hand goodbye,
release shapes numbered by the days in our hair,
give away with a poof of my fingers

a million hues turning gray & gaudy

(two piles of smoke)
(one passenger)
(zero tolerance)

I sit in orchid heat & wait
for genesis mud to cover me
with confident shoulders.

Afternoon Affair

He is Thirty. Big Tom. 6'4. Tan.
He is Fifteen. Little Sam. 5'7. Green.

He is father's Pal. Buddy. 32. Swell.
He is father's Pal. Buddy. 15. Shell.

He is Married. Sold. Gold. Bass.
He is Single. Sale. Silver. Tenor.

He is Lindsay's. Husband. 33. Fine.
He is Mother's. Son. 16. Fine.

He is Post. Workout. 5K. Glow.
He is Mid. Homework. 1st Century. Whoa.

He is Sleeping. Beauty. 4:12. Den.
He is Jungle. Book. 4:13. Kitchen.

He is Snoring. Mooring. 4:14. Peak.
He is Curious. Serious. 4:15. Peek.

He is Growing. Showing. 4:16. Boxers.
He is Growing. Showing. 4:17. Briefs.

He is Rock. Stock. 4:18. Sugar.
He is Mouth. South. 4:19. Salt.

He is Wink. Nod. 3-2-1. Heaven.
He is Lip. Sip. 1-2-3. Heaven.

He is Hush. Now. 1-2-3. Hell.
He is Mush. No. 3-2-1. Hell.

He is Smoking. Camels. 4:45. Leave.
He is Eating. Crow. 5:00. Stay.

Location (and the Lack of) Motivation

This town, my town, the one
you left for his town, which
starts with an A, unlike our town,
which ends by a dump behind a
stoplight blinking red as if to warn
indecision of every yellow light at
which we yielded to kiss & eye-gaze
& whisper *so happy*, & at every
green light we rushed through like
freebirds and cheered like so. Good.
Lights illuminate your absence, pole
frequencies mounted on new plots
with new facades with new names
in this town which carries on in the
middle of my life as I pray for utopian
claws to rapture me from our hues
faded by cyclone cessation. Or maybe
it's the other way around. No matter,
alteration has embossed me with stick pins
& I have never stepped into, or out of,
Depends. Blue is the color honeymooner's

engrave in this town, my town, the one
you left for his town, which ends
with an Z. Everyone knows paint fades,
which is why I sit in the hair salon in a
crunchy vinyl chair & let Susie foot-
pump me up until my Viking roots fall
from her blonde fingers turning a platinum
ponytail into a light-brown tonsure worn
by morose sufferers in mourning, imploding
when she asks if your career has yet found
fulfillment and have I booked our next
travelling-abroad destination. Yes and no, I reply,
as if I see and talk with you in this town,
my town, the one you left for his town,
which rhymes with muchacho and gazpacho.
I can still smell you in Denny's coffee,
Costco samples, Lund's bakery shelves,
Target dollar bins, Kwik Trip bananas,
& DSW clearance racks. I can still touch
the tops of things you touched when we were
we—mainly my hands, my pride, my lips,
my rose, my sores. I go everywhere yellow
& still end up blinking red.
How's your friend
doing these days? Everyone asks.
Some days I starve & scream.
Often I drive barefoot to the library
one town over, its windows

hanging like purpose on a cliff
where I Google ancient cities without
stoplights & check out cook books
about French cafes & stab red flags
onto laminated coral reefs shrinking
in African waters on a map trapped
like monotony in the corner of an
off-white wall cruising overnight
through The Castro, Fiji, Greenland,
Provincetown, and the London Eye,
awakened by bombast television fog
& a necropolis of bills I can't afford
to pay from a checking account in my name,
in this town, my town, the one you left
for his town, which takes three hours
& costs sixty dollars to reach by
noon & has an antique car museum
& a 60-minute narrated boat tour highlighting
architecture marvels twinkling the lakeshore,
including the newest six thousand square foot
villa carved into sandstone a year ago
by a businessman and his husband
who moved from a dump of a town,
I hear, to this town, the guide tells me,
one of the TOP 20 towns in America
where lucky people in the startup of love
call, and have called for years, home.

Fiddler

A week later,
pine tree scent
still in our bones,
jingle bells
still in our crotch,
hot cocoa
purring in the mixer,
bare skin hanging like dandy
fanciness easily triggered,
I find you in bed,
hairs and shadows,
ROOTS on television
      (yes master)
How deep, I think.
How egalitarian and
open-minded and rare and soft
      (yes master)
I jump on the mattress,
scare you into attention,
I like my men
on high alert.
This movie is spec-tack, though

not a New Year's Eve pick for most.
Why today? Why now? Why this? Why me?
To remind us, you say,
how well we have it
as white, rich, American men.
We laugh.
I stop.
You don't.
No way.
Sorry, it's true.
Silence screaming between
metric breathing.
No. No. No. No.
Not another ruler.
Not another arrow.
Not another intercropper.
Not another ornament I must put away,
forever.

Riverbed

receding. my one perfection.
dry muscles sinking inside chairs that
creak from loner poundage.

wrinkled sofa cushions. bed sheets
unamused by the temperature
of stretched skin and mood shifts.

vanishing. the grotesque landscape.
the darkened blemishes. the cracking,
snapping eardrums. the iciness

hardening vertebrae. the stingers
dropping ten-fold below under-privilege
replete of memories that burn in the sand,

among the land, which no one sees.

A Hui Hou Kakou

Kanaloa, god of the water,
here is your sick man...

Fingerprint-friction
wheeled the transformation,
one second chained to mind-cuffs,
another second adrift

in wing-dipped baptism
without some pastor-panhandler
messing up my hair.
But there was submersion and

I did hold my breath,
brought in perhaps by the
first grade waves
I plotted as a chubby-acne-

poor-trailer-trope
below a red crayon moon
bleeding for connection
in the top left corner.

Maybe Poseidon twisting
in the sea coughed
up a treasure chest
with crown & scepter to

quiet the seaweed storm
twisting in me. Hawaii in
boyhood fantasies was
padded by catalog contours

and cartoon sketches for skinny,
zitless, rich, mansion, hotties.

Yet there I stood, leaning
against your colossus masculinity
inside The Cheesecake
Factory lobby in Honolulu,

catching a force-fed
reflection in a lei-framed
mirror morphing in
real-time thirty-year

taboo: nascent-mist
to abstract-swell
to venture-tide
to expansion-shell

to fresco-shoreline
to watercolor-skies.

I release you,
the mirror whispered.
I wish I had snapped
a picture—finally

a souvenir worth
keeping—and told you.
I believe you'd have smiled.
Perhaps you'd have cared.

Housing Fragments

on odd little tables
    cheap quietness

layers like trinkets past pains
numbed by mood stabilizers and psychotropics
fused with intermittent toilet twitches—

so long body and mind: goodbye breakdown of trust:
hello bait my hook and rout seasons from my eyes:

    may I tell you a secret?

I was seventeen when I first cried
moon-day tears of disenfranchisement,
lounging face up on a polyester sofa,

soaking in dystopian projections of orientation

from true believers doubting my discipline to reject
(sun/son/sin)light and other rainbow configurations
travelling down roads that once, then not at all,

lost visibility to
fogginess, silencing

my lips from talking:
my hips from walking:
my quips from flocking:

like a queer
STOP IT! WE MEAN IT!

softness turning rancor
into a garden of rattlesnakes—

what pressure my blood was under,
cells draped in concentric compounds
with inquinate skin cloaked in passing days.

The Lion, the Peacock
and the Changeling

I'm an eagle, squint and perch,
ogling shadows
scuttling across your
new living room window,

you're a lion, hair plugs and girth,
he's a peacock, spikes and squirm,

we're all transmogrified
by shifts abiding in hiding.

Adjustment is painless for some
and unbearable for others—

A minute ago, parked beneath
a dead streetlamp, I was
a parrot with a rubber beak
and retrospect eardrums

listening to memories flash
in kaleidoscope images
of us as a couple of doves,
coo and advent, in flight.

Parrots are such
unreliable narrators—

Redbull ether churns me
like a cheetah aching to sprint,
to pounce, to pierce
and to rip out your (and his) throat.

Lion veins with minced
peacock heart sounds delicious—

Shadows embrace, espousing
scents, bare chests
tightening the knot
breaking us farther apart,

tangling me into the network
of reinvigorated jealousy.

Now I see things as they
have come to be—

As a hyena, I crouch
below the open window
in predator-creep
and inhale paint

fumes drying on a wall
you said my
imagination was
spinning out of control

silly boy, tricks are for kids—

"I've never felt this
strong for anyone," you whisper.
"I didn't know joy
could feel this good," he whispers.

As a Pitbull with snarled fangs,
I drip saliva onto shattered glass.
You look up, shake your main,
point the peacock downstairs,
pop out your chest and face the maze.

"You have thirty seconds
to leave or I'm calling
the police, you weak freak."

> *Am I weak because*
> *you call me a freak?*
> *Am I strong because*
> *you call me weak?*

A hurdling deer.
A flying white-rumped Swift.
A shelled snail.

A louse—

Driving to another
friend's couch
in a car payment
three months behind,

I try to not count ten
shelters and eleven
basements synonymous
with chicken shit.

The Age of
Blissfulness Was

your first introduction was
my curing in your name was
your lusting to see me tomorrow was
my leeching off your forest neck scent was

strolling the Stillwater pier was
interlocking pinkies was
booking a river boat cruise was
cuddling as fireworks chalked the sky was

a picnic conversation about sharing was
a county title at Ozark Trail North was
a master suite with an oceanic alarm was
a backyard grill with tiki-torches was

Big Marine Lake oak dock was
Passat Peggy's joint lease was
Polaris four-wheeler helmets was
Adirondack chairs in firefly dreams was

history we didn't anchor was
apologies we didn't improve was
secrets we didn't repeal was
monogamy we didn't respect was

darkness is what we believed it was
alchemy is what we doubted it was
venom is what we bottled it was
eradication is what we conferred it was

Agent Conclusion

The fat sidewalks in town
still squeeze thin footsteps

below the shop where you
worked as a seamstress,

illuminated with Jalapeno-lights
poking and stitching as

television cloudiness flicker
on bar-height counters

decades after Father muttered

NO THANK YOU & GOODBYE

my body lined with burrs, and you,
Mother, the smell of cedar,

the rage of rayon, the plight of dye,
running in a circle of Camels.

Willpower

Center Confessor

Runched up like grubs,
we defamed each other, considered it time well spent

devouring ammonia, cyanide, and sewage
freeing our enslaved hearts from the monster

masks handcrafted by injected scrim:
everything else is provisional,

east to west, collected, aged.
The wide skull of young gazelles

denounce women, *contra naturam*, pried
open by splayed hands, quite unappealing,

and you're a stickler for solstices
and I'm thicker than any brick,

—filthy baggage, reloaded—
our tiny ritualism fires made of

sugar, jam jars, and oriental spices.
You were the floor and I was the foot that trod

the door in the attic, swelling in some weather,
I crossed the street, scraping the balls of my feet,

to appear illusory

walking through a cloud of yellow moths
with little magic escaping.

Ice Cream Spot

Its depletion angered my emptiness,
less than two scoops of Deluxe Vanilla

clinging to bucket sides & hiding out in
bottom obscurity around highbrow neighbor-

hood flavors—Rocky Road, Seaside Surfer,
Candy Cane, So-So-Superman, Bubble Gum.

Like ew, a teenage girl said to another. *Nobody
wants leftovers. Why don't they just throw it*

*away and start over? Only somebody
totally desperate would order it. Ga-ross.*

I'll take the rest of the Deluxe Vanilla, I said.
Seems at one point a lot of people wanted it.

No Independence Day

Step into plaid and triangle shapes

canvassing water's bark, knees disappearing
from a concentric wind calling for my

spine to collapse and elbows to sink
—hurry up already—chest-high in

Hmong, do-rag, and hijab children
racing in jest at the far end of the lake in

inflatable alligators, clowns, turtles, and
ninja warriors as family units assimilate

like praise-hounds at the finish line (leaving
for a spell ragged picnic tables laved with

sweets): finger-calling mothers and deep-
bravado fathers and grandma Dorothy

and gramp-gramp Lewis and auntie Yusor
and uncle Pheej screaming GO! GO! GO!

And I can't absorb the laughter, the winning
names, the finger-snapping squeals of delight.

No more phoneless, textless, meaningless
holidays. No more firework shows, memorial

day monuments, turkey, ham, champagne
toasts, Valentine's, St. Patrick's. And the

immersion brings bubbles and depth and
the antidote is a glorious display of submission

into wetness when a voice uplifts the madness
—I love you dada and mama—

scattering the animus scaremongers
warring beneath the waves summoning

midnight fracas to drown daytime drought.

From/Hear

because / I
couldn't / translate
his / higher

UP

I / found
someone / FASTER
who / could

DECODE

my / sliding

DOWN

because / there
is / no

language / ONLY

communication / landscape
rolling / as

ENORMOUS / silence

The Institution of Final Admittance

Now that you can marry, will you, she asked,
the only neighbor throwing it out there.

This long together, it feels like we are, I said,
the only neighbor throwing it out there.

If you mean to each other, than no, you said,
the only neighbor throwing it out there.

Breakfast for Dinner

Family week...

       bring your baggage: square zippers, plastic
       locks, lip-clench woes, and loose-fit humor

cards to help mask any tears the preset schedule rule-

       book makes trueness shed layers of padding
       from the storehouse of invisible limbs we carry like

bones, the fancy-man therapist stresses pairing-sharing,

       except we first have to eat at 6:15pm and it's
       my chore to belly-fill fellow rehab(itants),

family factions...

       meatless spaghetti my specialty—not again—
       my mother chimes in with a hot hand for

whisking large pizza-size pancakes I can still sniff asleep,

       stargazing at being the sort of son she and father cheer
       for and high-five neighbors who respect my skill-style-

pride brimming with golden-hour moments eclipsing

      future failures inch-pinching ahead because
      gold wins favor and champions pay elation forward
      and selling precious metals is a cognition tragedy mother
      wraps sliced potatoes in aluminum foil ruffling on
      the grill, bacon popping in a skillet, strawberry syrup

family recipe…

      sprite boys tip-toe through kitchen aromas and
      nod as father flicks like rough scales fingernail

grease with a parry knife onto the floor at which he growls

      in length as if stamping disapproval on this horror house
      he drove me to hang up my doubt that conversion therapy

can change the divide God—and man—crossed between us,

      mother calls for the troops to set the table and who wants
      orange juice or tea or coffee she bought from a filthy

Venezuelan because no one likes American wimpy-pansy crap

—oh mom—and the meal is a slam dunk no joke no heads
no tales as the therapist swishes like crazy town
in a baseball cap and pink pants and says,
"you're up in fifteen" and the mood drops
like eggs sliding down a gullet because fifteen
means three hours of eyebrow-gymnastic
reproach listed on a two-faced whiteboard

family dysfunction…

bouncing more shame in this jungle gym
we have all vaulted to perfection,
although none of us are winners,
just limp   (delirious)

imps chewing on mother's farmhouse culinary craftiness,

      as father finishes swift, and firmly Bible-bundles
      himself in robes of rectitude to scripture my gay
      out of this crookedness straightened only by the
      nails & loincloth of Christ who raises the price tags on
      mother's four ex-husbands and wrist-heavy nephew Ricky,

not father's most excellent alpha and omega morality upbringing

when the therapist crosses both legs and with sweet-lip
lisp-honey says, "relative truthfulness
must own their defects

in this serious condition of self-debauchery" infuriating father's

courtship with lies and challenges mother's need
for deep-voice stoicism points me upstairs to repack in a
polka dot suitcase the little I brought to room three of six

steps because what more does a queer need in a condo of queers

than one dapper desire to squash through pathos, pretense,
and parade-promises indeterminate
kinked stages ridding the

pathway of faggotry forever from eating away at every

family meal...

6720

I cycle to breakthrough an invisible
barrier where dedication mirrors direction

      whether one mile out

or   two hours in(cline)
or   fifty seconds from finishing

the one hundred and forty

      heartbeat (pace+race=face)

or   maybe it's nothing less than insanity winding down
or   maybe it's little more than weekday persistence

working a brain dogged to reawaken two
wheels that never take me far enough

      to realize habit is so much more than pastime

but the submission (at some point) to a journey
    of blistered toes & a kinked neck
    & prostate spasms & mind-fuck discharging

        scale-wow-nourishment at the finish line
               (sometimes)
    between 11-2   (because I know)

    inexplicably   after all the sweat:

      legs take me to the end—
walls keep me at the beginning—
    surrender leads me to equilibrium
    spinning in the middle—

Twenty Odd Steps to Becoming Another Ill-Fit Rejection

This job's a circus troop under a dome.
Two high wire acts. Three riggings.

Four stars. 5. Take plastic stairs to
      metal scaffolding to the

          CEO's air-bending lair. Wow.
          Now this is a vaulted ceiling.

   SIX: I should mention—
           I will mention—
           I have to mention—

7. If I believed one-third
of my self-assertions, I'd have three
quarters more or less self-doubt.

8. I am (not) professional.

   I am (not) currently employed.

   I am (not) targeting companies.

   I am (not) picky. AT ALL.

NINE: Is a benefit a benefit
if it denies the benefactor the benefit?

10. Some of my skin's
brightness has dropped anchor.
11. Some of my cell's
synergy is disconnected.
12. Some of my references
come from embellished tribes of ingenuity.

THIRTEEN: (nodding repeatedly)

YES. ABSOLUTELY. FOR SURE.
GOT IT. OKAY. MAKES SENSE.
AH. COOL. GREAT.

14. "I bought this new tie. Nice, right?"
"It's okay. We're pretty hip here."

15. Did I misread my own coolness?
    Do I not look hip?
    Does my face transmit out-of-date?

SIXTEEN: 0-4 hours parking = $10.00
(cash only). SHIT >>>>>>>>> Do you validate
parking? Do you accept checks?

17. The hungry mouth
    to feed is mine.
18. The county shelter is
    becoming a real bus-ride probability.
19. NOT a loser. NOT a loser. NOT a loser.

    TWENTY: Loser

Critical (LIT)MUST Test

make love in prose
cook in poetry
decorate in memoir
converse in non-fiction

&

practice in short-story
forgive in flash fiction
respect in epic novel
share in novelettes

&

kiss in revelation
hold hands in exposition
laugh in proliferation
hug in composition

&

phone in 1st person
text in 2nd person
tweet in 3rd person
mail in 4th person

                    &
lust in mystery
        binge in romance
                snack in sci-fi
                        fill in history
                    &
exercise in verbs
        bathe in nouns
                dress in adjectives
                        labor in adverbs
                    &
discover in gestalt
        give in hubris
                ask in verisimilitude
                        pray in exegesis
                    &
hope in present tense
        dream in past tense
                exist in future tense
                        love in everlasting motif

Guider Drive

I wasn't nimble enough to climb
the calcifications linked to your spine,

nor ride the whiplash roller-
coaster clocking your fists,

nor crawl from beneath the
stairwell your public persona

mocking my rooftop, marking it
unsealed, silly, spacelessness.

Men's Balls are
So Commodified

Men's balls are so commodified.
In sport nuts mount an own-it theme.
How round the world is testes tied.

Tap long balls scoring from behind.
So experts screech on FIFA screens.
Men's balls are so commodified.

Foot, golf, soft, base, cue, blue, hard, wide
is open game for love machines.
How round the world is testes tied.

Are cheers for balls that fall ringside
more Sontag grab than Craig-stance scene?
Why are men's balls so commodified?

Venues are built for balls slick-slide.
Fans worship balls with bellarmine.
How round the world is testes tied.

So clap for a sack or hangout with pride
or cream a man's balls for a baby's dream.
Man's bells are so commodified.
How round the world is testes tied.

Nationality Reformation

I smell cumin-clove ethnicity
before taking a side-swipe glance
at her Iranian configuration:
Miss Abaya-body-dress in open-toe

sandals stomp-jogging on a treadmill to
the left. She is anti-me and I am anti-her,
although I speak with an unbiased tongue
hinged to equal-seeking meat-packing bones.

PC means POLITICAL CLOUT.
IRAN means INSURGENT RADICALS ACCOSTING
NONPROLIFERATION.

I read The Onion. And Time. And Tehran Times.
I've been marginalized for years. It's unfair
being an outlier, even if my bias sees through
color-chart whiteness. Which thrives. Here.

Axe body spray boosts capitalism's creed.
GO-USA t-shirts promulgates indigenous first.
I never wonder whether foreigner
acclimation empowers exclusion

or whether rebellion defends attachment.
I come to the gym to run and sweat,
not to contemplate expat affiliations.
She laughs: robust and plucky,

shocking my space pleasure.
Aren't woman from lesser cultures
supposed to hold tight their lips

IN THE COMPANY OF MEN?

I follow lash-brown eyes to a television
hanging by chains from the ceiling
playing on AMC the movie
Julie and Julia, the point in

the plot where Julie fist-holds
a sliver-tip knife while Julia
demonstrates how to debone a duck.
It's funny stuff. I laugh. Beside her.

"Have you seen the entire thing?" I ask.
She does not instantaneously answer,
scanning my face as if to authenticate both
the genuineness of my tone and its question.

"No. Do you think it's at Redbox?"
Her Un-American accent needles my jingoism.
"Probably," I say. "Which one do you use?"
"The McDonald's by Valley Creek Mall."

"The Walmart by Becker Furniture has two."
"Does it? Maybe I'll go there next time."
She pushes the red off button, quiets the
looping belt, finishes the twenty minute trip.

"Happy cooking," I say. Suck it, ISIS.
"An Iranian woman in Midwestern America
cooking French cuisine. Now there's a movie,"

she says. We make eye contact and nod, snubbing,
for a tick, humanity's picketing predilections.

Conditions of the Race

deep inner poverty
causes some men

to thread
deficiency through

a series of glazing,
theatrical night sweats

while in other men
deep inner poverty

proves self-deprivation
thrives in a new series of lies

Rebranding

Nobody wants Sheepshead Wrasse for dinner,
until the chef renames it Labridae Luxoticca.

The sad Obese Dragonfish doesn't make the
top of a shopping list—but CapaDapaMapa does.

The Tassled Scorpionfish has a frightening
overbite but rechristened it Pink Pacifica

and watch its culinary popularity catapult.
Squirrelfish may put you off, but how about

Baha Beritorous? Sounds delicious, right!
Change Bulldog Stargazer to Redtip-Roughy

and customers will overprize it, right into a
ten-percent harvest rate in seafaring waters.

Caribbean Melty (AKA: Indo-Pacific Red Lionfish)
makes the endangered list, too. As does Kume

(AKA Red-Spotted Blenny). It's true, catchy
titles sell. So no, we are not Slimy Sculpin, a

white, mild, flaky, fly-fish caught in the waters
of Lake Superior; we're Coupler Cloverfish, a

most delectable tropical dish served with a side of
passion fruit to consumers marinating in adoration.

#VH1TVONTHURSDAY ATEIGHTOCLOCK

Eleven eleganza All-Stars on
RuPaul's Drag Race are hiding out in
the interior lounge drinking Absolut
Vodka during a commercial break.

#teamtrixie

Heidi Klum needs a pair of undies.
Finding Prince Charming isn't a choice.
Cenegenics engenders age (and sex) defying ascendency.

#youremissingit

snoring two sofa cushions over,
head dipping like a bobber,
lips twitching like Milli Vanilli,
belly bulge like a papa bear
holding a striped brown

pillow I tossed in the
trashcan yesterday—hated it—
which you dug out and fluffed today—loved it—
which is a problem, your optimism, that is,
your penchant need to
revive things I consider dead.

#equivocationmuch

I can count with scrupulousness your flaws:
 1 pen-cap cyst on your left cheek.
 2 funky toenails.
 3 rolls of chin blubber.
 4 nose hairs.
 5 dollar can of mixed peanuts from Big Lots.
 6 chocolate chip cookie crumbs on your shirt.
 7 cherry-vanilla Pepsi bottles.
 8 cigarettes.
 9 age spots triangulating your face.
 10 ten, a big fat hen...cock.

#lifetimefitnessmaybe

I know why
You sleep
> Without masks
> Or concealer
I know why
You cook
> Without weights
> Or scales
I know why
You argue
> Without names
> Or games
I know why
You care
> Without fear
> Or falsehood

#contentmentrealness

The All-Stars are shooting
eye daggers and lace panties at the crowd.
The luminary fairies are snapping back.

#thestruggleisreal

The season finale ball gowns cheer for,
and with, costume-ovation hysteria.
And the winner is (you ready to lip sync for your legacy?)

#ohpitcrew

A cannonball blasts kaleidoscope confetti.

#youremissingitagain

I think you are neither my
fast drag nor my ideal race.
Goodbye mister-interesting-as-lukewarm-mustard.
I trust when you awaken my absence will prove

#iamsilentlycorrectingyourdreams

Determination's Path to Redo the Did

The Executive Director
banished me from the premises,
punishment for
staining the needlepoint teacher
with *bitch*, who smeared
my story-arc-narrative
in front of stranger-classmates
as unliterary pornography
(looking back, it is).
My bad. My tongue. My face
illustrating with a frown
the stomach-pain lesson of
think-before-you-speak
and how-old-are-you-anyway
and you're-not-
welcome-here-anymore.
And I wept, not exactly
for the teacher, although
her victim-tattle did squeeze
an apology from my chapped lips,

but for the deficit of joy
the premises afforded me
and my notebooks, with
its high-rise windows and
picture-clown walls and
scuff-marked floors and
a jazzy café with Jasmine tea.
Yet I followed the ban
like a missing person sequestered
from worse, and better, places,
asking myself how does mistake
inform crassness that penance
over time can restore foul-mouth
to Listerine ting; that no one is beyond
redemption; that I, even in my
recklessness, am worth a closer
look if only to model the distance
between immeasurability and substitution.
No threats. No retaliation. No finger blame.
No rolling tears. Or eyes. Or dice.
Just shoulder the ban and
write less pornography elsewhere.
One year. Two year. Three-and-a-half years.
BREAKING NEWS: The Executive Director
is moving to Birmingham, replaced
in a color brochure by a tall,
tweed-suited woman with hairy arms.
My shelf-life jumped, buzzed, and cheered.

My neck and knees popped back into place.
My wish for restoration sat
on both shoulders and twinkled
like a VIP. I signed in online,
used a real name, wondering
if the new director's nose
sought out past mildew.
One day. Two day. Three-and-a-half days.
A confirmation email touting
full participation. Approved.
Publically endorsed. Yes. Indeed.
We're back, sang anxiety, doubt, and isolation.
We've been forgiven, said depletion's heaviness.
And I wept, not exactly for the new teachers,
classes, and story delights,
but for your, and my,
unliterary pornography
(looking back, it is)
with its high-rise windows
and picture-clown walls
and scuff-marked floors
and a jazzy café with Jasmine tea.
But wait, if reestablishment
can happen here, it can
happen anywhere, to anyone,
dare I say it: to us

Not Everyone
is Embracing
the Shift to Sunshine

i can cure yOu

oF affirmAtion
    of beatifiCaTION
              OF compoSure
              of daylight
of expOsition
    of formULa
                 Of generosity
           oF Helium
   of idEals
       of joculArity
          of kisses
   of luminosity
of memoRy
    of nuance
              of ouTdoors
   Of pragmatism

oF QUeriEs

                of reST

OF soBernEsS.

                        of treaTs.

OF underutiLizatiOn.

        of Virility.

            of wishEs.

OF xerophthalMia.

of yondEr.

                      OF ZIP.

It is What It is

Your response,
regardless the conversation,

is metallic evenness,
a robot doing robot things,

staring vacuously at my
dumb puns, quips, and cues,

speaking nothing beyond
the encryption, "Hmm."

Nightfall Mastication

uphill sleep is hard, dear one,
god knows, satan too, that
   change climbs
   during darkness,

so love yourself brightly, sweet one,

   let youthfulness-orange drift

among handsome blue-eyed boys (or girls)
grazing with hyper-civic zeal
   upon gingerbread-red-
   headed girls (or boys)—

slumber squirt is too small for us,
for me, for you, kind one, even

   a slight squeeze

will unclose
& unlatch me,
mystery covering

flesh cuts (or bruises)

    so please

peel the wet-thick-
glaze of acceptance

    & absorb me, soft nectar,

bring me close to mouth-lust,
let me dance & thrust
& jump & whistle
    because a smell can alert
    movement & sound

to find the permanent (re)calling of
synchronization, believe me, loved one,

swallowing the mountain down.

If Only

Self-centered enough
to keep your attention.

Self-realized enough
to give you away.

Self-confident enough
to take you back

and make
us better.

Emotion

Trainspotting

Guitar-string hairs shoot like
angry bed head above a booth at

    KFC: you've shrunk, a hat

man you are not, embarrassed
neither by raggle-taggle twigs

    nor dinnertime choices,

a quadragenarian with a pension plan,
a miser on a budget of pedant means

    which helps explain

your meanness, oh hell, you're obsceneness.
Yet I fall like flight for your inkwell eyes

    & slip like grease

for your bedlam lips & sit across
MedSpa wrinkles drawing like wind

your desert hands

clasping a yellow soda deprived of ice:
we gobble the silence, the only meal

our immensity has ever shared.

Supersex Linguist

Fusing, judder and ossify, green-blue
eyes steaming in a crisp-face-husk: German

jawbone commandeering lips—*Männlichkeit*—hunger
fueling the grind, slop-sizzle tongues

licking size, salt, and sea.
Sie sind so verdammt sexy, you

whispered, edging me closer to
incentive twist, bear, and drain—

newness never getting old—
magnetism reaching combustion—

Dies ist so erstaunlich, so heiß.
I've never been talked to like this:

echoes my ears can't conceive: foreign
textures wrapped in unbalancing shapes:

Ich muss dich Wiedersehen.

Fingertips drawing definition across
hairline, eyebrows, nose curves, & neck veins.

What did you say? What does it mean?
Ich werde gut zu dir, wenn du gut zu mir sein werde.

We lingered. Enraptured. Caged. Absorbing

through every pore in my bed every syllable
seeping from inside and outside your head.

Concentration is the Game, Keep the Rhythm

Twelve spoons from IKEA
      for bachelor nation (forced viewing)
         nestled between

butter knives & salad forks, first cousins
      with weedier, lumpier jobs. A week later,
         eight. Less. Gone. Runaways. Stolen.

Who pilfers flatware from Swedish cabinets?
      Check beneath the sofa cushions. Inside
         the dishwasher floorboard. Behind the bed
frame.

Eight's fine. Ten's a cliché—mankind's
      idealistic expectation of attaining perfection.
         Seven, heavens number or not, carries

such middle management confines, led by some
    caffeine-addicted-wraith who swooped
        in while I was dreaming of being in

your wake & pushed coffee buttons &
    slid spoon(s) behind a skeleton ear &
        hummed "When The Saints Go Marching
        In," &

floated like steam through
    a chink in the kitchen window—
        proof to vengeance that vice

demoralizes vitriol. Six. Five. Four.
    Rake the carpet behind the television.
        Sweep linoleum below the sink.

Rummage the trashcan—good lord—spoon three
    stuck head-first in a key-lime yogurt.
        Wraiths take many forms. And I am their
sleepwalker.

Dazed. Nights. Spindrift. Hail.
    Marked in majuscule black.
        Impinged by hide and seek.

Time Zones in
the Petting Zoo

A cockroach is born to hate.
I know this is true because a
cockroach told me as much.
I was born to hate, he said.
I'm impressed by self-assessment.
I do not possess the reward of
insight. I am a follower,
a mosquito, pest and flicker.
We met on a Tuesday night at
a karaoke bar in downtown
Minneapolis, Minnesota.
A bare-chested gala for men only.
Inhibition plastered the walls.
Freedom laced the drinks.
Be yourself hung like blood
brothers infusing each other
with sweat, rum, and trick-or-treats
in the bathroom. The cockroach
told me to follow him to the stage
and sing with him his favorite song:

Joan Jett's *I Hate Myself For Loving You*.
A song we sang for eleven years.
Real crowd-pleasers. A two-for-one
bargain: mister hate and mister-sister.

Midnight gettin' uptight, where are you?
You said you'd meet me, now it's quarter to two...

The cockroach was born premature,
blind, and wingless. Birth defects.
Unrepairable flaws. Daggers that
stabbed his life long before death.
Before we'd sing, he'd tell a joke:
What do you call a blind, wingless
cockroach standing on stage
with a microphone in his hand?
Pause. *Better than a mosquito.*
The place lit up. Wild applause.
He made people happy. I wish
he could have seen the smiles.

...Hey Jack, it's a fact they're talkin' in town,
I turn my back and you're messin' around...

I was fond of the cockroach's
thumbnail-size-broad-
level-body and pin-needle
head. I told him as much.

Give it a week, he said.
After two weeks, I stopped
saying it, asking instead
about parents and siblings.
Nothing and no one, he said.
I asked about fears and goals.
Darkness and wings, he said.
I asked about hate and love.
Hallelujah and no way in hell.

> *... I'm not really jealous, just
> don't like lookin' like a clown.*

Before we met, I hung with
a caterpillar who mocked the
very idea of transformation.
A chameleon who despised
changing color. A hyena
who detested meat. A tapir
who so thoroughly disliked
being a tapir, he wore an elephant mask
and called himself Zesty, the circus
elephant. Sad, I thought,
despising your own kind.
Not one of my ex-friends asked
if I wished to be something other
than a mosquito. Which I didn't,
and still don't. Though many say I should.

121

A Burmese cat is born to love.
I know this is true because a
Burmese cat told me as much.
I was born to love, he said,
at a Starbucks on a Sunday,
while I was on a caffeine run for
the cockroach who was whining
in bed about being hung over,
dry, and bored out of his mind.
I made the huge mistake of telling
the cockroach about my encounter
at Starbucks with the Burmese cat.
The cockroach stood on his back feet
and spewed from chapped lips a
hot load of yellow-green bile that
covered like web-netting my body.
I got a searing fever. Thank goodness
it was raining outside, where I
stood for an hour and let the wetness
cleanse the burn. Later that night,
at the karaoke bar, I thought a lot
about my old friend, the tapir,
who died of a searing infection
due to complications from AIDS.

The cockroach took the
stage without me, told the joke,
and sang the duet by himself.

...hey man bet you can treat me right,
you just don't know what you was missin' last
night...

The cleansing rain brought
two serendipitous revelations.
One, I wanted to stay clean and
two, I wanted to sing karaoke
with someone else. I never
spoke to the cockroach again.
Sometimes I miss him.
Sometimes I wish I'd have
asked him to come outside
and stand with me in the rain,
and let it wash away all the hate.
I try to imagine what he'd
look like as a Burmese cat.
I only saw the Burmese cat once,
but once was more than enough
to teach me a thing or two about love.

...I think of you every night and day,
you took my heart the way you took my pride
away...

The cockroach often bragged
about living in a rent-free,
fully-furnished condominium
which he came to inhabit
from a wasp who needed to
move out, and onward, after
a Deathwatch Beetle had
cheated on him with an ant.
Wasp's are stupid and silly,
the cockroach said, *And
born to do what they're told.*
The cockroach and I sat
quiet for a very long time.
Then, laughing sinisterly, he said,
*Breakdown is the value any cross-subsidized
economy loses in order to make things change.*
Wow. It's true, when you think about it.
I figure that's why he owns one hundred
wind-up clocks, each one set to chime
on the hour in Central Standard Time.
I know about the clocks because I
helped shoulder, and carry, many of them.
I also helped him wind (and rewind)
each one inside his (and mine for a while)
condominium. I guess that's why
I felt comfortable to ask him
three questions about time.

1. *Do clocks repeat the past or solidify the future?*
2. *How long have you been spewing bile?*
3. *Are you guilt-ridden for exploiting the wasp's heartache?*

Huge error. He pushed me out the front door,
stood on his back feet, and spewed on my
body another load of yellow-green bile. Then he
hissed and called me the ugliest mosquito ever.

> *...I hate myself for loving you,*
> *can't break free from the things that you do...*

Today I live with a diamondback
rattlesnake, a real-estate-tycoon
who I met on specieshookupdotcom.
I was born to buy and sell, he said.
I moved into his two-story house on
Pebble Lake after dating him for a week.
Rent-free and fully-furnished. I'm lucky.
He had no idea how close I was to sleeping
on the floor at the local animal shelter.
I was born to love you, I tell him.
Which is a lie. Which he tells me back.
Which may be the truth. Or a lie.
He hates karaoke. Which is fine.
I'm adaptable. I don't need to sing,
even though I do love to sing.
Yesterday, after we finished

shopping for PRIDE tattoos, I saw
the cockroach carrying another
clock. I told the rattlesnake
about my past involvement
with the cockroach.
OMG, he looks so hateful,
the rattlesnake said.
And why does he keep
bumping into everything?
Is he blind or something?
OMG, is he wingless, too?
What a fucking mess.
I can't believe you
were ever friends with
a cockroach. Is there
something wrong with
you that you haven't told me?

    ...I wanna walk, but I run back to you,
    that's why I hate myself for loving you...

Tender Slip

After years of bruising against Father's elements

    (fire, air, water, and earth)

Mother fell into a humdrum waking coma

    (for keeps)

carrying the burns to church

hiding the welt-chills at the meat counter

drowning in the floodlights removed from the closet

dying like a flower pressed in the
pages of a thick, wordless book

    (mournful cries)

Posturing

You kept me at the precise
distance of one misplaced word,

one disagreeable sentence,
one criticizing opinion

damning you long enough
to run the other way and

write deletion upon extinction.
And you were quite fulfilled. I too kept

you at the precise distance of one
misplaced word, one disagreeable

sentence, one criticizing opinion
damning me long enough

to run the other way and write
deletion upon extinction. And I was

quite fulfilled. Giving each other colonization-
ineptitude along dirt roads of lip service confinement.

Shadow Shifting
Sensations

At the grocery store, squeezing
oranges, lemons, beer brats

and barbeque meats, I hear
your chit-chat overloading a cart.

We were never engaged like that.
Never piled on layers of dialogue.

Never pickled in pleasantries.
Never checked expiration dates.

Or filters.

At the sports store, experimenting
with Saucony tennis shoes, Adidas

shorts, Brooks t-shirts and toes socks,
I see your polyester man purse

hanging like femininity around his neck.
We were never fags like that.

Never wore matching Fitbits.
Never shared a water bottle.

Never modeled runway mesh
for a clerk with a textbook ass.

And social currency.

At the hardware store, gathering
charcoal, matches, logs, a sleeping

bag, and a tent, I smell your
devotion to Bird of Paradise cologne.

We were never strong like that.
Never sizzled with aftertaste.

Never burned with inferno rage.
Never let one phoenix rise to the top.

Or bloom from the bottom.

At the park, reflecting ponds, fronds,
swing sets, and monkey bars, spreading

a sprinkle of breadcrumbs to the geese
we named Sam The Sham & The Pharaohs,

I miss the names we whispered
when accusers weren't checking boxes.

We were never nurturers like that.
Never picked from or fed off the land.

Never circled in succession.
Never content to wait our turn.

In any straight line.

Carter Michael

Decades younger,
he shares Shauna,

my sister, his grandma,
who can't explain in a

Chucky Cheese birthday
text why she loves

his great-eight so much.
Or maybe she can. Try.

Maybe it's because
she loves me, too.

Root for the underdog.
Cheer for the oversight.

The fatherless.
The gay.

The outsider who so
much wants to be in.

Come Home,
Ex-Ex Gays

Dear Fellas of the 26th Street Fright Nights,
I am here. I am rested. And I am less afraid of
mixing colored markers with self-empowerment.

Oh, how the fanatics tried to strip our fairytales,
to straighten our curl, to replace natural oil with
boogieman rubbish laced with godless lies—liars—

Wrong is wrong. Right is now ours to Grand. Slam.

I took up sewing, interweaving multi-color,
multi-dimension, and multi-grain
into a superhero suit (with sequin cape)

come through—

touch flex-cool carapace repelling
all flamer-hater shade

smell lavender-laced lining embedded
with razzle-dazzle polyglots

watch phantasmagoria stilettoes
catwalk body-beautiful ascots

come on, good Judy—

applaud the purling takeoff:
whistle the rollicking flightpath:
ace the coruscating landing pad:

I'll sew one for you, if you promise
to never let anyone steal its exquisiteness.

I Instagram, Tweet, and Post. Send a message.
I will respond. We are not cesspool smut.

We cannot pray DNA away.
We belong to a family whose history
is enriched by our membership.

Sashay, saunté, my dear, you stay.

Oppositional
Woundedness

Leaving the echo of mourning,
which of us will replay the booming

promises we failed to keep sound

and which of us will rewrite the
crashing gong of collapse we seceded

by engaging new accompanists.

Two Days Before Cancelling Disneyland

The fever sweat out the confession:
the infidelities, the lunches, the overnights

my ass and lips riding on the half-hour
the tingle of another man's kiss,

another man's insignia, another man's
home, another man's bed unprotected

from pollutant streams on which I drifted,
doggie style, raindrops pounding the window

while one football team pummeled another.
How could I have done this, I do not say,

and you do not ask, two thermometers
laying like lie detectors beside my ears

as you read from the Disneyland pamphlet

Mickey and Minnie's noontime pageant,
Cinderella's Castle, Goofy's cupcakes, and

a pinch of pixie dust makes everything
old new again. Then you fall asleep,

freeing our grip, returning to the plot in the
folklore where aspiration thrives, faithlessness

endures, and nirvana marches in stride.
Then you awakened and I dialed

the clinic for an appointment,
your face deactivating when

I whispered in the receiver *multiple times,*
red flag symptoms, high chance of risk.

I had never before heard you whisper God's name.
Or beg him to spare us from living in my hell.

Sing the Words Below
to the Tune of
My Favorite Things
from *The Sound of Music*

Kisses bring upswing and hugs uplift downtime.
Lists in your notebook plus cursive retracing.
Driving to Hudson and walking the pier.
Snacking on dark fudge from John Belvedere's.
When the sun beams. When the wind moves.
When I'm feeling sad. I simply remember my favorite
things and then I don't—cut don't—feel so bad.

Writers Workshop

A Wednesday affair for fingers with pens to
scribble an autograph and up to 13 pre-paid minutes

on a postcard dropped like a selfie in a manila
envelope, *The Hat*, picked with randomness

by a month-long moderator who pounds a gavel
at seven-thirty to drive a team of story arcs

seeking publication to read into a microphone
character wears from a hot seat that takes

critique to adjournment by nine-thirty. A bright-
light-schedule for dreamers. Someone always has

more shade to add. Or subtract. Edit is the
razorblade whoremaster in this game. We play.

I worry for The Hat's digestive system, forced
to eat our concoctions, much of it compost.

I distrust joy that comes from binging on cardstock
only to purge it within minutes. I know what seedy

past-matter rewritten by future aim tastes like.
Tell me we haven't made The Hat bulimic.

Or obsessive-compulsive, conditioned by
ritual greediness seeking to be heard,

respected, validated, flattered, loved.
Oh, how we tease The Hat with fullness,

trying to prove the notion of saturation
bringing completeness to emptiness. How long will

The Hat keep falling for our mania? One look at it is
to find a ratchet hairpiece with whuffle-pinched lips

laying with locked flatness inside a suitcase for six days:
one hundred and sixty-six hours a week. No wonder its

frailty looks so jaundice. Not everyone treats it well.
Some people refuse to acknowledge disease.

Some people are sicker themselves. Some
people like to ram a hand into powerlessness—

sour spores implanted with failure.

I'm glad The Hat spits them out first, fast, and
foremost, ridding its gut of unsavoriness,

holding longer to signatures bearing milk-fat,
mincemeat, tale-bone, story-wise, brave-heart.

The Hat knows the opposite of sustenance is
insubstantiality.
The Hat knows we are wearing it out, oftentimes with tears

we cannot fight and from shadows we have to give away.
So I coddle The Hat. I mend it with tape and staples.

I leave it face up inside the suitcase and try to help it
remember its calling. And the spiked trail of my name.

To You

Josef, who couldn't hear from his left ear, to you
Dennis, who renovated a lake house, to you
Grant, who immured veins with Tar, to you
Jerry, who called me Jeff, to you
Dan, who battled analogue monsters, to you
Nick, who left me holding two movie tickets, to you
Dean, who poked light into my scars, to you
Leo, who misunderstood ask for receive, to you
Gary, who hid every glass bottle, to you
Bryan, who honestly didn't care, to you
Soren, who also dated Gary, to you
Jay, who dreamed of breaking chains, to you
Jerome, who hated being sixty-one, to you
Mark, who begged to sleep over, to you
Carl, who refused to sleep over, to you
Marco, who signed my name in the sauna, to you
Dale, who force-fed equanimity, to you
Jon, who stole cashmere mittens, to you
Kris, who believed in praying it away, to you
Brian, who bought me a ring, to you
Justin, who made Maundy Thursday possible, to you
Wayne, who whispered gay is okay, to you

Jason, who flew an invisible plane, to you
Tim, who drew me close without even trying, to you
Meridith, who begged me to reconsider, to you
Josie, who reeked of deceitfulness, to you
Crystal, who readjusted perspectives, to you
Kurt, who gave without conditions, to you
Glenn, who conducted my heart, to you
anyone, who found me thumbing for home,
I am still in search of pagination-existence.

Joy

It starts with a J

which is 5 bets before O

which is 10 bets before (why)

I harp back to b (or not to be)

cuz

distance discursion distracts

everything, everyone, everywhere,

from finding

goddamn

(hmm)

it—

jesus…

Klonopin

Lidocaine

Muckracking

Nova Scotia

Orgasm

Purveyor Proliferating Pots Paraphernalia

Quelled

Revoked

Stymied

Through

Untenable

Vitriol

Whirling

X-ponential

Yearning yesterday, yesternight, yesteryear

Zipcodes

& it's true

3 of 26

becomes 6 of 52

which is closer to 55

than 45

and 36 is a fraction of 37

38, 39, then 40/60 understands

every clock is work

every after is thought

every self is worth

every joy is full

of emptiness

Reason Good as Any

Your love for
another man

doesn't render
me unlovable.

On the contrary,
it proves that

you can love,
which is much

closer to did
than didn't.

Liar

The sound of weeping is work,
so I load my handkerchief with delusion
and climb fast the blueprint velvety heart
beating beyond the clasp of your adventure bruise
feeding off sinewy embryos, and all my bones are in it,
the marrow being drained by the distinct
pleasure of your unbuckling, untucking, unfastening

and you practice like this
anyway, you fisherman of fraud,
you're right, you're right

I do not understand your bootlick-placenta
made of downcast eyes and biting quince
souring the mooring I can no longer find
through foggy bitters wrought
by the tangle of sickening rope-roots
coiling around me, choking the yes
I gave with an ambivalent no—
I should have stayed transfixed to no—your yes,
a large rot of smears plucking forever aftershocks

Senior Year
to Senior Year

I know I'm not the one you thought,
the one you hoped, the one who brought
God's great crown to pew and call
the one who sang in harvest hall

I know I'm not the one you sought,
the one you clapped, the one who caught
God's great hand to raise and pine
the one who prayed to fix the find

I know I'm not the one you want,
the one you lost, the one who got
God's great stain to curse and blot
the one who cried from every spot

the one who cries, who cries a lot,
who weeps for the one who knows he's not

About Samuel E. Cole

It began in the countryside where fourth generation farmers tilled the hardy soil exposed in large rectangles, outlined by poplars and jack pine. The old Swedish and Norwegian accents could still be heard in the tinkling voices of the elder women who gathered to weave rugs by hand. The sometimes terrifying solitude of the countryside and the beauty of a nature that would somehow spring up through a deeply frozen land profoundly formed Samuel's perspective.

Samuel E. Cole, a writer of prose and poetry, lives in Woodbury, Minnesota. His stories, poems, and essays have appeared in numerous literary magazines, including *Apocrypha & Abstractions, Literary Orphans, Foliate Oak, Pure Slush, Empty Sink Publishing, Breathe Free Press, Fix It Broken, A Few Lines, Second Hand Stories, Dryland Lit, Blackheart Magazine, Ascent Aspirations, The Write Launch, RFD Magazine, Flywheel, Dual Coast, Full of Crow, Diddledog, Rathalla Review, Image OutWrite,*

Storychord, Capra Review, Edify Publi-cations, Linden Avenue Literary Journal, Subtle Fiction, The Hungry Chimera, Storgy, Queen Mob's Teahouse, Identity Theory, Literary Yard, The Bookends Review, Nixes Mate Review, Winamop, and *Blink Ink.*

Cole's first poetry collection, *Bereft & the Same-Sex Heart,* was published in 2016 by Pski's Porch Publishing. His second book, *Bloodwork,* a collection of short stories, was published in 2017 by Pski's Porch Publishing. His third book, *Siren Stitches,* a collection of short stories, was published by Three Waters Publishing in October 2017. He is a key player in adding to the paper trail chronicles of The Minneapolis Writers Workshop and enjoys spending time and energy making memories with family and friends.

Learn more about Samuel E. Cole:

www.samuel-cole.com

www.facebook.com/coleport

instagram.com/samuelcole9853

Thanks

Special thanks to The Minneapolis Writers Workshop, especially Marc P, who is a champion of my work. And to Kurt Duex, for his unwavering support.

The following poems have been previously published:
'Cherry Horses', 'Instinct', 'Epiglottis', *The Write Launch*
'A Most Promising Boyfriend's Daughter's Perspective',
Truth Serum Press
'The Beginning Stages of Connecting the Dots', *Jazz Cigarette/Petrichor*
'Afternoon Affair', *Drunk Monkeys*
'Empty Vessels', 'Location (and the lack of) Motivation',
Poetry Circle
'The Institution of Final Admittance', *Weasel Press*
'Supersex Linguist', *White Ash Literary*
'The (UN)Musicality of Miscellaneous Romance', *The Almagre Review*
'From/Hear', 'Men's Balls are So Commodified', *Wanton Fuckery*
'No Independence Day', *2018 Minnesota Voices Poetry Series Finalist*

Also from TRUTH SERUM PRESS and PURE SLUSH BOOKS

https://truthserumpress.net/catalogue/

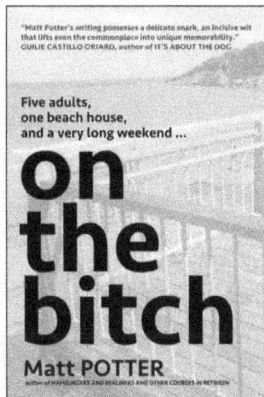

- *Kiss Kiss* by Paul Beckman
  978-1-925536-21-8 (paperback) 978-1-925536-22-5 (eBook)
- *Happy²* Pure Slush Vol. 15
  978-1-925536-39-3 (paperback) 978-1-925536-40-9 (eBook)
- *On the Bitch* by Matt Potter
  978-1-925536-45-4 (paperback) 978-1-925536-46-1 (eBook)

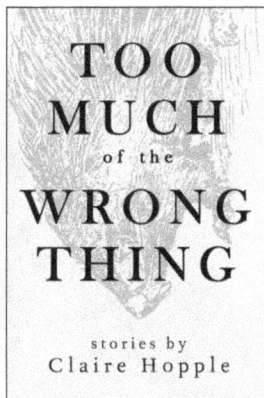

- *Inklings* by Irene Buckler
  978-1-925536-41-6 (paperback) 978-1-925536-42-3 (eBook)
- *Lust 7 Deadly Sins Vol. #1*
  978-1-925536-47-8 (paperback) 978-1-925536-48-5 (eBook)
- *Too Much of the Wrong Thing* by Claire Hopple
  978-1-925536-33-1 (paperback) 978-1-925536-34-8 (eBook)

Also from TRUTH SERUM PRESS

https://truthserumpress.net/catalogue/

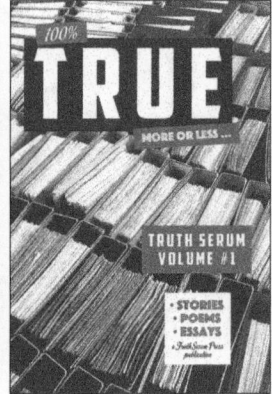

- *Track Tales* by Mercedes Webb-Pullman
  978-1-925536-35-5 (paperback) 978-1-925536-36-2 (eBook)
- *Wiser Truth Serum Vol. #2*
  978-1-925536-31-7 (paperback) 978-1-925536-32-4 (eBook)
- *True Truth Serum Vol. #1*
  978-1-925536-29-4 (paperback) 978-1-925536-30-0 (eBook)

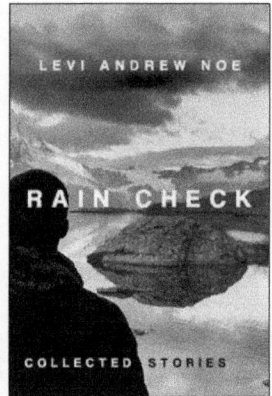

- *Hello Berlin!* by Jason S. Andrews
  978-1-925536-11-9 (paperback) 978-1-925536-12-6 (eBook)
- *Deer Michigan* by Jack C. Buck
  978-1-925536-25-6 (paperback) 978-1-925536-26-3 (eBook)
- *Rain Check* by Levi Andrew Noe
  978-1-925536-09-6 (paperback) 978-1-925536-10-2 (eBook)

Also from TRUTH SERUM PRESS

https://truthserumpress.net/catalogue/

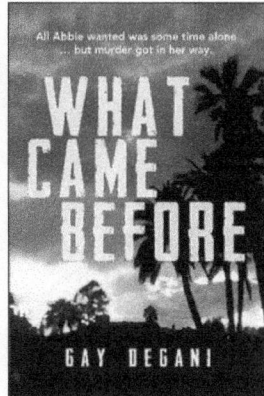

- *Luck and Other Truths* by Richard Mark Glover
  978-1-925101-77-5 (paperback) 978-1-925536-04-1 (eBook)
- *happyme@t.us* by Kim Conklin
  978-1-925536-07-2 (paperback) 978-1-925536-08-9 (eBook)
- *What Came Before* by Gay Degani
  978-1-925536-05-8 (paperback) 978-1-925536-06-5 (eBook)

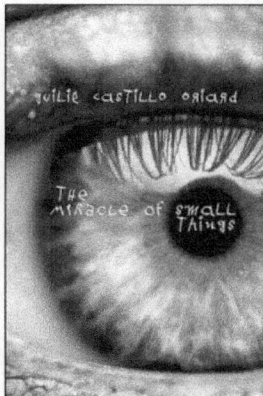

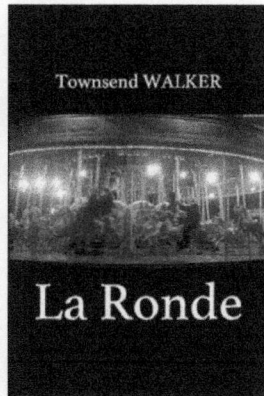

- *Based on True Stories* by Matt Potter
  978-1-925101-75-1 (paperback) / 978-1-925101-76-8 (eBook)
- *The Miracle of Small Things* by Guilie Castillo Oriard
  978-1-925101-73-7 (paperback) 978-1-925101-74-4 (eBook)
- *La Ronde* by Townsend Walker
  978-1-925101-64-5 (paperback) 978-1-925101-65-2 (eBook)

www.ingramcontent.com/pod-product-compliance
Lightning Source LLC
Chambersburg PA
CBHW030017290326
41934CB00005B/375